Quilt Notes

Everyone uses pot holders. Why not make yourse a set that contains one for each month of the year They should last a long time when they only get use for a month and will add a bit of decoration to your kitchen for years to come.

Make a couple extras to give away while you are stitching. When an occasion arises and a gift is needed, you will be ready with a much-appreciated gift as these pot holders are perfect for anyone.

Try several different appliqué methods, including freezer-paper, fused and interfaced appliqué, while using up some scraps from your overflowing scrap collection.

Remember to use cotton batting rather than polyester, as the polyester batting will not resist heat and can actually melt when used. Just because these pot holders are pretty doesn't mean they should not be used!

Meet the Designer

Barbara Clayton is a freelance quilt and craft designer. For 17 years her work has been published in such magazines as Quilt World, McCall's Needlework & Crafts, Victoria, Stitch 'N Sew Quilts, Country Needlecrafts, Doll World *and more. She has a Bachelor of Arts degree from Brigham Young University where she majored in art and minored in clothing and textiles. She has also illustrated the children's book,* Willy Whiskers, *by Beverly Labrum.*

Born in Florida to a military family, Barbara moved frequently across the United States and Germany. She first started quilting in Connecticut for her small children while her husband was out to sea on a submarine.

In addition to quilting, Barbara enjoys portrait and still-life painting, designing sweaters and doing genealogy. She is the mother of six children and now grandmother to three more. She lives in Castle Rock, Colo., with her husband and teenage son and the occasional college student returning home for a visit.

Annie's® Published by Annie's, 306 East Parr Road, Berne, IN 46711. Printed in USA.

Every effort has been made to ensure that the instructions in this publication are complete and accurate. We cannot, however, take responsibility for human error, typographical mistakes or variations in individual work. Please visit AnniesCustomerService.com to check for pattern updates.

ISBN: 978-1-59012-978-4

2 3 4 5 6 7 8 9

General Instructions

Although the pot holders are different shapes and sizes, they share appliqué and quilting methods. When making individual pot holders, you will be referred back to specific sections of these General Instructions.

There are three different methods of appliqué used to make the pot holders—fusible appliqué, freezer-paper appliqué and interfaced appliqué. Some projects use more than one method. Each method requires some specific steps. If you prefer to use another method for your version of these projects, please be sure that you have the necessary supplies before you begin. For example, if the project uses interfaced appliqué and you choose to use fused appliqué instead, you will need to add machine-embroidery thread, fusible transfer web and fabric stabilizer to your list of supplies needed in order to complete the project.

It is fun to have quilted projects to decorate your home, and these pot holders, designed for specific months of the year, are the perfect quilted addition to any kitchen.

Interfaced Appliqué

1. Prepare templates for each appliqué shape. Transfer cutting instructions for the chosen project or projects to templates.

2. Cut shapes as indicated on pattern piece for number and fabric color, adding a 1/4" seam allowance to each piece and reversing template to trace on the wrong side of the fabric. Cut an identical shape from medium-weight fusible interfacing for each fabric piece needed.

3. Place appliqué pieces right sides together with the fusible side of the medium-weight fusible interfacing pieces; stitch around seam allowance, using all-purpose thread to match fabric. Clip curves and trim points to a 1/8" seam allowance.

4. Cut a slit in the interfacing side of the stitched units. Turn each unit right side out through the slit using a knitting needle, pencil with broken lead or stylet to smooth seams and points.
Note: *Fusible side of interfacing should be on the outside.*

5. Draw any detail lines on motifs using a water-erasable fabric marker or pencil referring to the pattern for placement.

6. Prepare pot holder or oven mitt shape as directed in specific project.

7. Using drawings provided with each project, arrange the appliqué shapes on the background fabrics in numerical order. Iron in place with a medium-hot iron.

8. Cut a piece of fabric stabilizer to fit under the appliqué area or areas. Pin to the wrong side of the appliqué area or areas.

9. Using clear nylon monofilament in the top of the machine and all-purpose thread in the bobbin and a machine blind-hem stitch, stitch edge of shapes in place.

10. Remove fabric stabilizer when all stitching is complete referring to manufacturer's instructions.

Fused Appliqué

1. Trace pattern pieces in reverse on the paper side of the fusible transfer web referring to pattern for number to cut.

2. Cut out shapes leaving a margin around each one.

3. Fuse shapes to the wrong side of the fabric as directed on each piece for color; cut out shapes on drawn line. Remove paper backing.

4. Prepare pot holder as directed in specific project.

5. Using drawings provided with each project, arrange the appliqué shapes on the background fabrics in numerical order. Fuse in place with a medium-hot iron.

6. Cut a piece of tear-off fabric stabilizer to fit under the appliqué area or areas. Pin to the wrong side of the appliqué area or areas.

7. Using machine-embroidery thread to match fabrics (or as directed with individual projects if otherwise) in the top of the machine and all-purpose thread in the bobbin, and a medium-width machine satin stitch, machine-appliqué pieces in place.

8. Remove fabric stabilizer when all stitching is complete referring to manufacturer's instructions.

Freezer-Paper Appliqué

1. Trace appliqué shapes onto freezer paper using finished lines for tracing. **Note:** *No seam allowance is added to freezer-paper shapes.* Cut out on traced lines.

2. Press the freezer-paper shapes onto the wrong side of specified fabrics using a dry iron; cut out shapes, leaving a 1/4" seam allowance beyond edge of freezer-paper shape.

3. Fold the fabric seam allowance over the edges of the freezer-paper shape and press.

4. Using drawings provided with each project, arrange the appliqué shapes on the background fabrics in numerical order.

5. Remove freezer paper; machine-appliqué in place as in steps 8–10 for Interfaced Appliqué.

Rounding Corners

1. Make template for rounded corner using pattern given.

2. Use template to round three corners of pot-holder top, backing and batting referring to the project Placement Diagram for positioning of round corners.

Quilting

1. Sandwich batting between the completed top and backing pieces unless otherwise directed in individual pattern; pin or baste to hold.

2. All projects are machine-quilted close to the appliqué motifs using clear nylon monofilament in the top of the machine and all-purpose thread in the bobbin.

3. All projects are hand-quilted 1/4" around each appliqué motif and from project edge using quilting thread specified.

4. Hand-quilted detail lines and other hand quilting is specific to each project. Refer to project instructions for color of quilting thread and specifics for hand quilting.

5. When quilting is completed, trim batting and backing even with quilted top.

Making Bias Binding

1. All projects requiring bias binding list a specific number of yards of self-made or purchased binding. If using purchased binding, purchase a color to coordinate with the project.

2. If making self-made bias binding, purchase an extra fat quarter of a fabric used in or to coordinate with your pot holder.

3. Cut fabric strips on a 45-degree angle at 2" intervals for bias binding.

4. Join strips on short ends as shown in Figure 1 to make desired yardage as specified with each project for self-made bias binding.

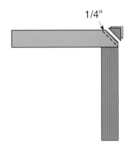

Figure 1
Join the strips on short ends as
shown to make desired yardage;
trim to 1/4" seam and press.

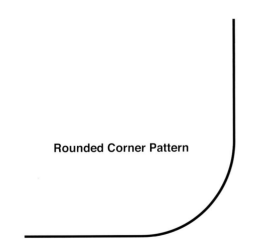

Rounded Corner Pattern

Applying Binding

1. For oven mitts, bind both top opening edges. Place front and back mitt pieces lining sides together. Baste around outside unbound edges.

2. For oven mitts and pot holders, place the bias binding right sides together with a top corner of the project. Turn in ends of binding 1/4" for oven mitts. Line up the raw edge of the binding strip

with raw edge of the project. Begin sewing at corner using a 1/4" seam allowance and all-purpose thread to match binding. Continue sewing around the pot holder or oven mitt until you approach the ending point of the project; stop stitching.

3. Cut a 2 1/2" tail at the end and enclose beginning raw end in binding strip; stitch to the end of the tail. Fold under end of strip 1/4" and fold tail to make a loop as shown in Figure 2, hand or machine-stitch in place to secure loop.

4. Fold under remaining raw edge of binding 1/2"; turn to backside. Pin or baste in place.

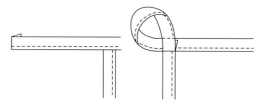

Figure 2
Fold tail to make a loop.

5. Using clear nylon monofilament in the top of the machine and all-purpose thread to match binding in the bobbin, machine-stitch in the ditch of binding seam on the right side, catching the binding on the back. ❖

January Snow Bear Pot Holder

Most bears hibernate in the winter, but our bear is weathering the storm on this wintry-scene pot holder.

Project Specifications
Pot Holder Size: 8" x 8"

Fabric
- 8 1/2" x 8 1/2" square blue print
- 8 1/2" x 8 1/2" square white solid
- Scraps green, brown and tan prints
- Backing 8 1/2" x 8 1/2"
- Cotton batting 8 1/2" x 8 1/2"
- 1 1/8 yards self-made or purchased white bias binding

Tools & Supplies
- White all-purpose thread
- Blue and white quilting thread
- Clear nylon monofilament
- Black 6-strand embroidery floss
- 1/8 yard medium-weight fusible interfacing
- 1/8 yard fabric stabilizer
- Basic sewing tools and supplies, stylet, knitting needle or pencil and water-erasable fabric marker or pencil

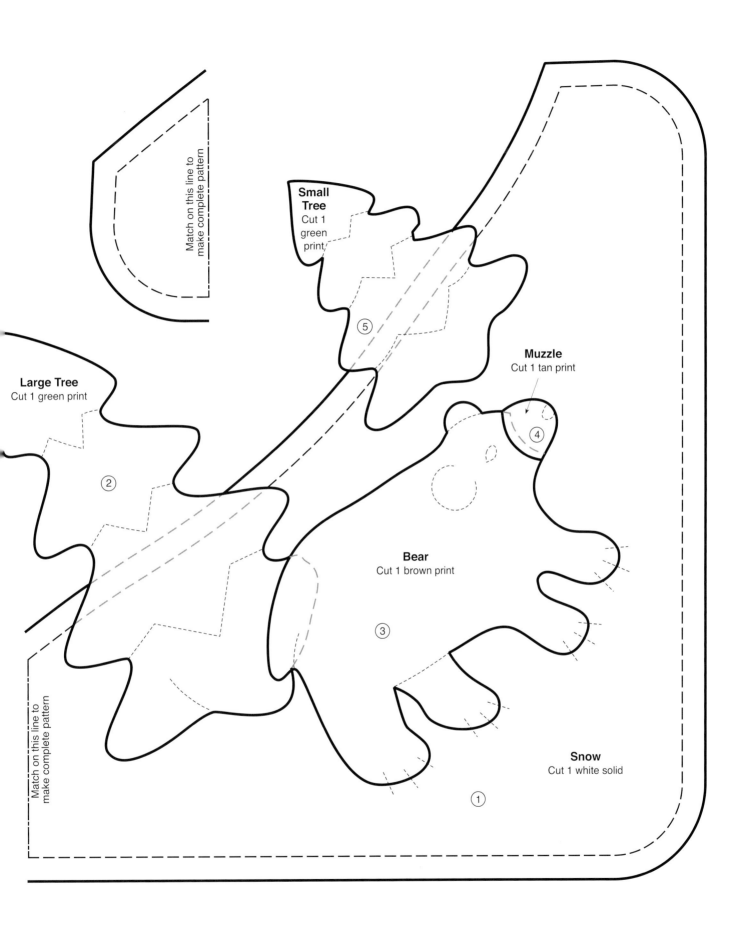

Match on this line to make complete pattern

Small Tree
Cut 1 green print

⑤

Large Tree
Cut 1 green print

②

Match on this line to make complete pattern

Muzzle
Cut 1 tan print

④

Bear
Cut 1 brown print

③

Snow
Cut 1 white solid

①

Snow Bear Pot Holder
Placement Diagram
8" x 8"

Instructions

1. Prepare templates for each piece using pattern pieces given; cut as directed on each piece.

2. Prepare bear and tree pieces for appliqué referring to Interfaced Appliqué in the General Instructions.

3. Round corners on blue print square referring to the General Instructions. Turn under curved edge of the snow piece and place on the blue print square matching bottom corners.

4. Machine-appliqué turned-under, curved edge of snow piece to the blue print square using clear nylon monofilament in the top of the machine and all-purpose thread in the bobbin.

5. Appliqué bear and tree pieces in numerical order referring to Interfaced Appliqué in the General Instructions.

6. Using 3 strands of black embroidery floss, stitch detail lines on bear as marked on pattern and using satin stitch for nose and eye, straight stitch for claws and running stitch for ears.

7. Prepare for quilting and quilt referring to the General Instructions using white quilting thread on the blue areas and on lines marked on trees and blue quilting thread on the white areas.

8. Bind edges, making a hanging loop, referring to the General Instructions. ❖

February Hearts Oven Mitt

Heart-shaped flowers make a delicate statement on a large oven mitt.

Project Specifications

Pot Holder Size: 8" x 11 1/2"

Fabric

- Scraps pink and green prints
- 1/3 yard each white solid and red print
- 2 rectangles cotton batting 10" x 13"
- 1 1/2 yards self-made or purchased burgundy bias binding

Tools & Supplies

- White and red all-purpose thread
- Green, pink and red machine-embroidery thread
- Dark green quilting thread
- Clear nylon monofilament
- 1/8 yard fusible transfer web
- 1/4 yard fabric stabilizer
- Basic sewing tools and supplies

Instructions

1. Prepare templates for heart and leaf shapes using pattern pieces given. Prepare pieces for appliqué referring to the Fusible Appliqué instructions in the General Instructions and patterns for number to cut.

2. Prepare template for mitt shape using pattern given. Cut three white solid and two batting; reverse and cut one red print.

3. Arrange appliqué shapes on one white solid mitt shape referring to the lines marked on the pattern for positioning of shapes; fuse in place.

4. Machine-appliqué shapes in place using machine-embroidery thread to match fabrics and referring to the General Instructions. Using green machine-embroidery thread and a medium-width machine satin stitch, sew stem lines as marked on pattern.

5. Draw diagonal lines 1 1/2" apart on one white solid mitt shape in both directions to make a grid as shown in Figure 1; sandwich a batting piece between the marked white solid and the red print mitt shapes and pin layers together to hold.

6. Using white all-purpose thread, machine-stitch on marked lines.

7. Sandwich the remaining batting piece between the appliquéd mitt top and another white solid mitt shape; pin to hold. Quilt referring to the General Instructions using dark green quilting thread for hand quilting and stems. Machine-quilt close to stems and appliqué shapes using clear nylon monofilament in the top of the machine and all-purpose thread in the bobbin.

8. Place the two quilted mitt shapes with wrong sides together; baste around outside edges.

9. Bind edges, making a loop on the thumb side, referring to the General Instructions to finish. ❖

Figure 1
Draw diagonal lines 1 1/2" apart
on the back white mitt in both
directions to make a grid.

Oven Mitt

Leaf
Cut 6
green
print

Large Heart
Cut 2 pink print

Medium Heart
Cut 1 pink
print & 2
red print

Connect on this line to make complete pattern

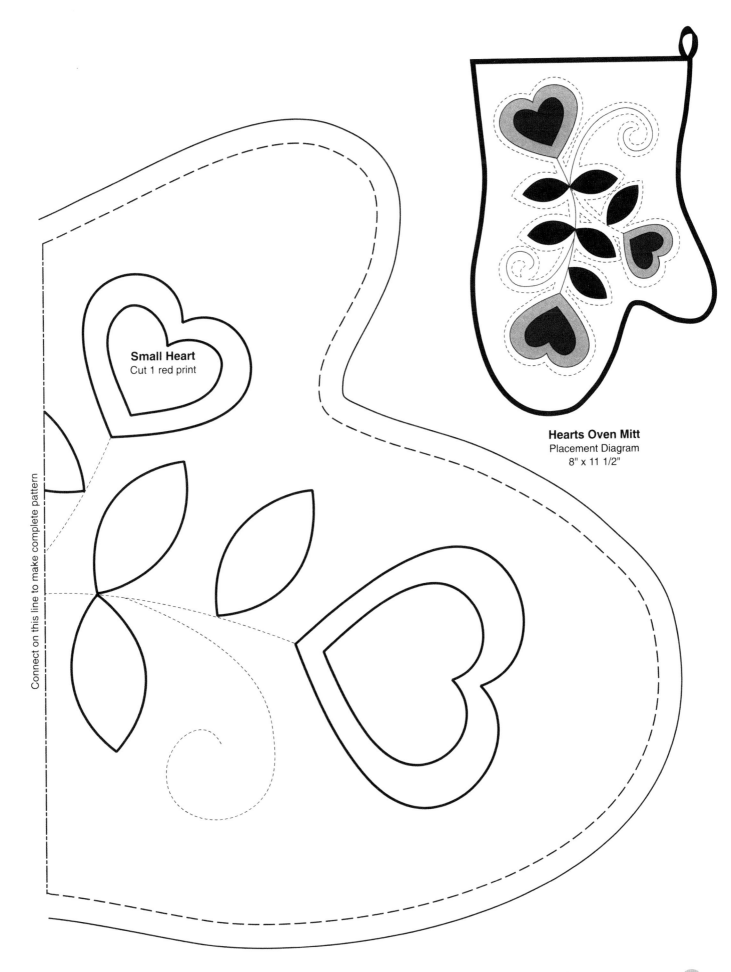

Small Heart
Cut 1 red print

Connect on this line to make complete pattern

Hearts Oven Mitt
Placement Diagram
8" x 11 1/2"

March Lucky Shamrock Pot Holder

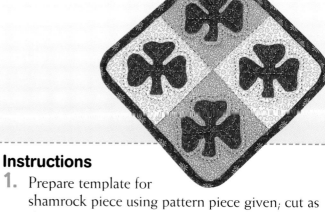

Simple shamrock shapes appliquéd to a Four-Patch block is enough to add the luck of the Irish to your March kitchen.

Project Specifications

Pot Holder Size: 8" x 8"

Fabric

- One 9" x 9" square each light, medium and dark green prints
- Backing 8 1/2" x 8 1/2"
- Cotton batting 8 1/2" x 8 1/2"
- 1 1/8 yards self-made or purchased green bias binding

Tools & Supplies

- Light and dark green all-purpose thread
- Dark green and white quilting thread
- Clear nylon monofilament
- 1/8 yard medium-weight fusible interfacing
- 1/8 yard fabric stabilizer
- Basic sewing tools and supplies, stylet, knitting needle or pencil and water-erasable fabric marker or pencil

Instructions

1. Prepare template for shamrock piece using pattern piece given; cut as directed on the piece.

2. Cut two squares each 4 1/2" x 4 1/2" light and medium green prints.

3. Prepare shamrock pieces for appliqué referring to Interfaced Appliqué in the General Instructions.

4. Join the squares to complete the pieced top referring to the Placement Diagram for positioning of squares.

5. Round corners on pieced square referring to the General Instructions.

6. Appliqué shamrocks in place referring to Interfaced Appliqué in the General Instructions.

7. Prepare for quilting and quilt referring to the General Instructions using white quilting thread on the shamrock shapes and dark green quilting thread on the background squares.

8. Bind edges, making a hanging loop, referring to the General Instructions. ❖

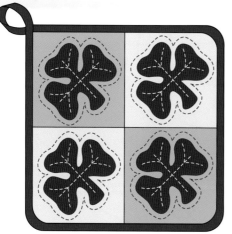

Lucky Shamrock Pot Holder
Placement Diagram
8" x 8"

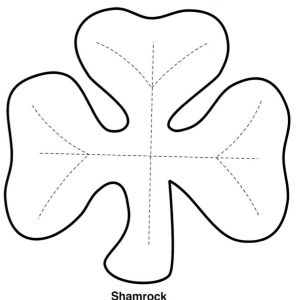

Shamrock
Cut 4 dark green print

April Bunny Pot Holder

This Easter Bunny will be happy to help you celebrate the Easter holidays.

Project Specifications

Pot Holder Size: 8 1/2" x 9"

Fabric

- Scraps light pink, pink, green, blue and yellow prints
- 3/8 yard white solid
- Cotton batting 11" x 11"

Tools & Supplies

- White all-purpose thread
- Gray and white quilting thread
- Yellow and pink machine-embroidery thread
- Clear nylon monofilament
- 1/8 yard fusible transfer web
- 3 1/2" x 3 1/2" square medium-weight fusible interfacing
- 1/4 yard fabric stabilizer
- Freezer paper
- Basic sewing tools and supplies, stylet, knitting needle or pencil

Easter Bunny Pot Holder
Placement Diagram
8 1/2" x 9"

Instructions

1. Prepare templates using pattern pieces given. Cut the bunny and egg pieces as directed on the patterns. Cut the egg stripe and triangle pieces and prepare for appliqué referring to Fusible Appliqué in the General Instructions.

2. Transfer detail lines onto the top bunny piece.

3. Cut and prepare the ear piece for appliqué referring to Interfaced Appliqué in the General Instructions. Place on bunny piece referring to the pattern for positioning, fuse and stitch in place, again referring to the General Instructions.

4. Cut and pin a 2" x 2" square of fabric stabilizer behind the eye area. Using pink machine-embroidery thread in the top of the machine and all-purpose thread in the bobbin, machine satin-stitch the eye shape; when stitching is complete, remove stabilizer.

5. Apply the stripe and triangle pieces to the eggs, again referring to the General Instructions. Pin fabric stabilizer behind each egg shape. Machine-appliqué shapes on egg pieces using yellow machine-embroidery thread on eggs 1 and 2 and pink machine-embroidery thread on eggs 1 and 3 referring to the Placement Diagram. When stitching is complete, remove stabilizer.

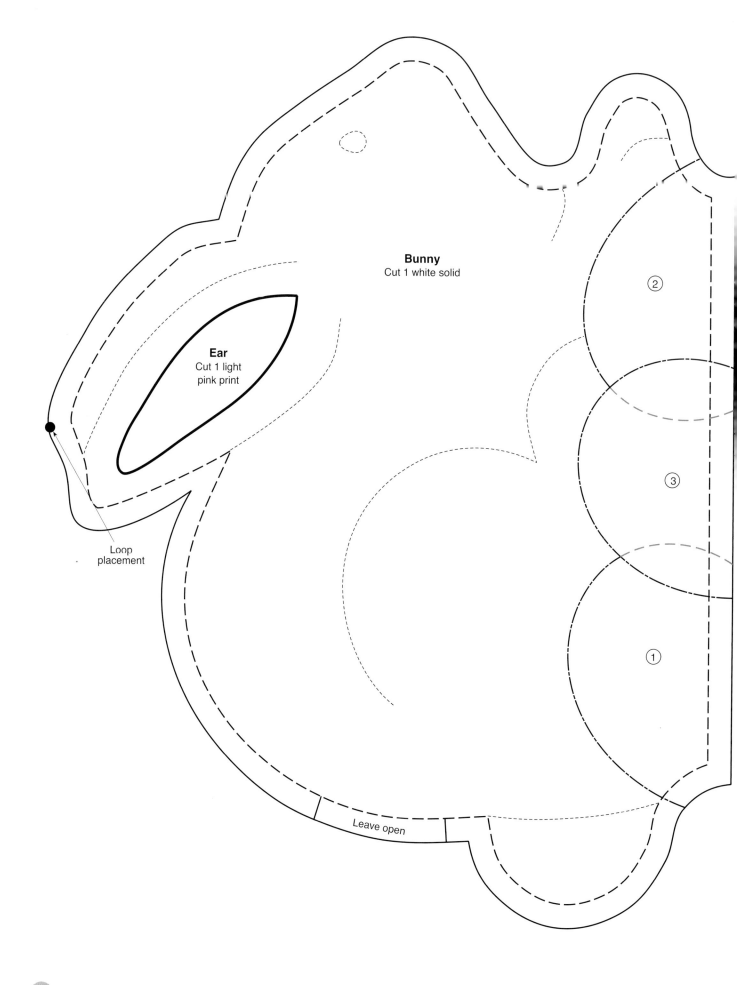

Bunny
Cut 1 white solid

Ear
Cut 1 light
pink print

Loop
placement

②

③

①

Leave open

6. Prepare egg shapes for appliqué and appliqué in place on the bunny shape in numerical order as marked on the pattern referring to Freezer-Paper Appliqué in the General Instructions.

7. Unfold the seam allowance on outside edges of eggs and press flat. Cut a white solid backing and batting piece using bunny-and-egg shape as a pattern.

8. Cut a bias strip 2 1/2" x 5" from white solid; fold in half and press. Fold the two raw edges inside toward the fold; press. Topstitch the strip with white thread close to the edge. Fold the strip into a loop and pin the raw ends to the top of the bunny piece as marked on pattern.

9. Pin the pot holder top to the backing piece, right sides together with backing shape; pin the batting to the backing piece.

10. Sew around the outside edges using a 1/4" seam, leaving an opening as marked on pattern. Clip curves and indentations and turn right side out.

11. With a stylet, knitting needle or pencil with broken lead, smooth out seams on the inside. Pull the loop up; slipstitch opening closed. Press lightly.

12. Machine-quilt around ear using clear nylon monofilament in the top of the machine and all-purpose thread in the bobbin. Hand-quilt around top edges of each egg shape and along the detail lines using gray quilting thread and 1/4" from outside edges using white quilting thread to finish. ❖

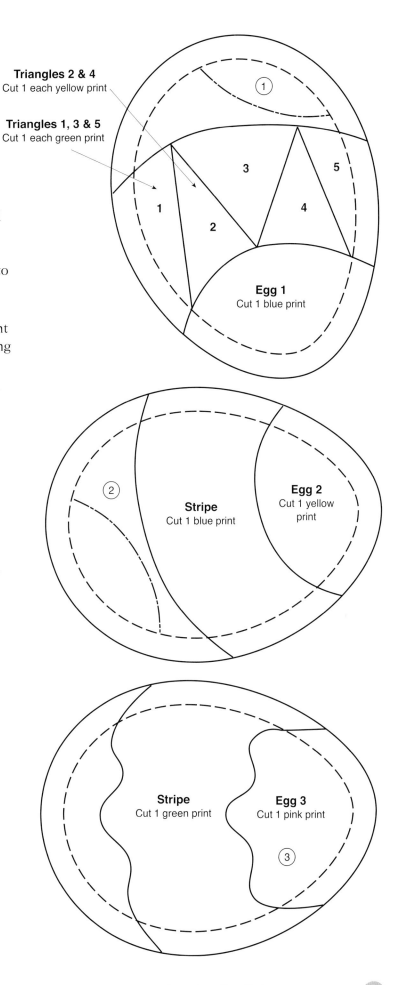

Triangles 2 & 4
Cut 1 each yellow print

Triangles 1, 3 & 5
Cut 1 each green print

Egg 1
Cut 1 blue print

Stripe
Cut 1 blue print

Egg 2
Cut 1 yellow print

Stripe
Cut 1 green print

Egg 3
Cut 1 pink print

May Spring Tulips Pot Holder

Swing into spring with a pieced-and-appliquéd, tulip-motif pot holder in bright spring colors.

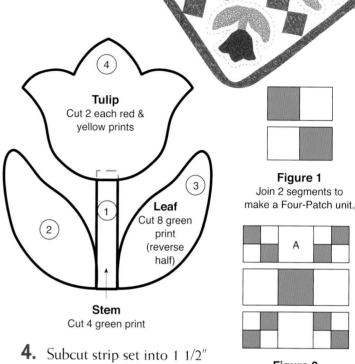

Project Specifications

Pot Holder Size: 8 1/2" x 8 1/2"

Fabric

- Scraps red, yellow and green prints
- 1/8 yard blue print
- 1/4 yard white solid
- Backing 9" x 9"
- Cotton batting 9" x 9"
- 1 1/8 yards self-made or purchased blue bias binding

Tools & Supplies

- Blue and white all-purpose thread
- Blue quilting thread
- Clear nylon monofilament
- 1/8 yard medium-weight fusible interfacing
- 1/8 yard fabric stabilizer
- Basic sewing tools and supplies, stylet, knitting needle or pencil and water-erasable fabric marker or pencil

Instructions

1. Prepare templates for tulip motif using pattern given; cut as directed on the pattern.

2. Cut one square blue print and four squares white solid 2 1/2" x 2 1/2" for A.

Spring Tulips Pot Holder
Placement Diagram
8 1/2" x 8 1/2"

3. Cut one strip each blue print and white solid 1 1/2" x 13". Sew the strips together along length with right sides together; press seams toward blue print strip.

Tulip
Cut 2 each red & yellow prints

Leaf
Cut 8 green print (reverse half)

Stem
Cut 4 green print

Figure 1
Join 2 segments to make a Four-Patch unit.

Figure 2
Join the A squares with the Four-Patch units in rows.

4. Subcut strip set into 1 1/2" segments; you will need eight segments. Join two segments as shown in Figure 1 to make a Four-Patch unit; repeat for four units.

5. Join the A squares with the Four-Patch units in rows as shown in Figure 2; join rows to complete an Irish Chain unit. Press seams in one direction.

6. Cut two squares white solid 5 1/8" x 5 1/8"; cut each square on one diagonal to make triangles. Sew a triangle to each side of the Irish Chain unit; press seams away from the triangles.

7. Prepare tulip motif pieces for appliqué referring to Interfaced Appliqué in the General Instructions.

8. Round corners on pieced square referring to the General Instructions.

9. Appliqué tulip motifs in place referring to Interfaced Appliqué in the General Instructions.

10. Prepare for quilting and quilt referring to the General Instructions using blue quilting thread.

11. Bind edges, making a hanging loop, referring to the General Instructions. ❖

June Citrus Oven Mitt

Prepare your summer picnic dinners using this pretty citrus-design oven mitt.

Project Specifications

Oven Mitt Size: 8″ x 11 1/2″

Fabric

- Scraps light and dark orange, yellow and dark green prints
- 1/3 yard each white solid and light green print
- 2 rectangles cotton batting 10″ x 13″
- 1 1/2 yards self-made or purchased light green bias binding

Tools & Supplies

- White all-purpose thread
- Green, orange and yellow machine-embroidery thread
- Green quilting thread
- Clear nylon monofilament
- 1/8 yard fusible transfer web
- 1/8 yard fabric stabilizer
- Basic sewing tools and supplies

Figure 1
Draw diagonal lines 1 1/2″ apart on the back white mitt in both directions to make a grid.

Instructions

1. Prepare templates for citrus shapes using pattern pieces given. Prepare pieces for appliqué referring to the Fusible Appliqué instructions in the General Instructions and patterns for number to cut.

2. Prepare template for mitt shape using pattern given on pages 10 and 11. Cut three white solid and two batting; reverse and cut one light green print.

3. Arrange appliqué shapes on one white solid mitt shape using layout of design given as a guide for positioning; fuse shapes in place.

4. Machine-appliqué shapes in place using machine-embroidery thread to match fabrics and referring to the General Instructions.

5. Draw diagonal lines 1 1/2″ apart on one white solid mitt shape in both directions to make a grid as shown in Figure 1; sandwich a batting piece between the marked white solid and the light green print mitt shapes and pin layers together to hold.

6. Using white all-purpose thread, machine-stitch on marked lines.

7. Sandwich the remaining batting piece between the appliquéd mitt top and another white solid shape; pin to hold. Quilt referring to the General Instructions using green quilting thread for hand quilting.

8. Bind top edge of each layered mitt shape.

9. Place the two quilted mitt shapes with wrong sides together; baste around outside edges.

10. Bind outside edges, making a loop on one corner, referring to the General Instructions to finish. ❖

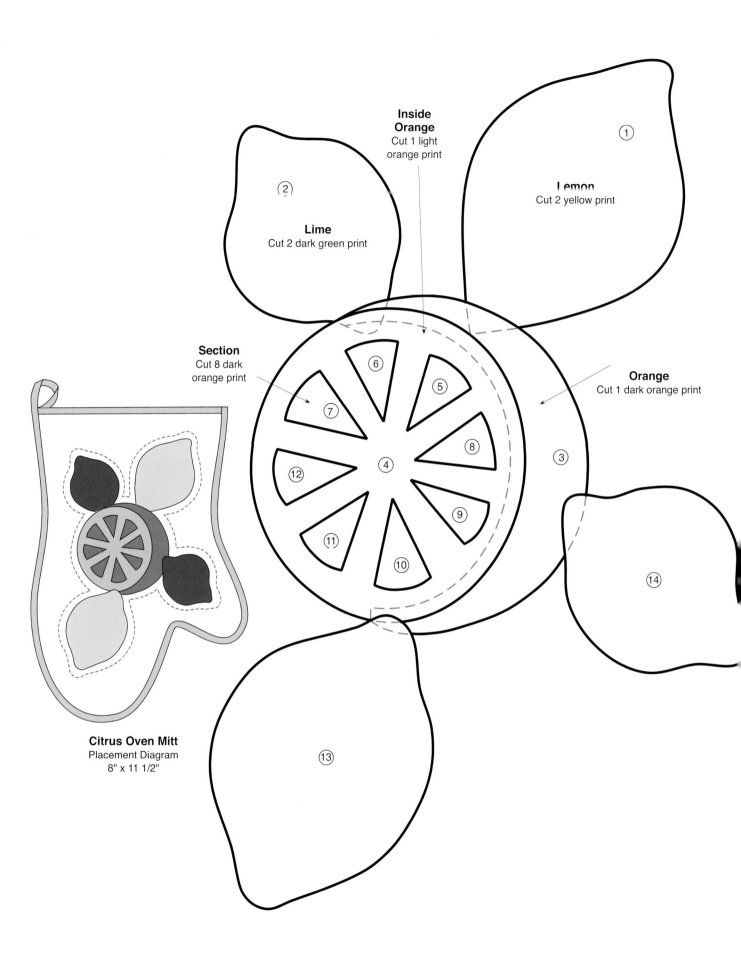

Inside
Orange
Cut 1 light
orange print

② (circled, faint)

Lime
Cut 2 dark green print

① (circled)

Lemon
Cut 2 yellow print

Section
Cut 8 dark
orange print

Orange
Cut 1 dark orange print

⑥ ⑤ ⑦ ⑧ ④ ⑫ ⑨ ⑪ ⑩ ③ ⑭

Citrus Oven Mitt
Placement Diagram
8" x 11 1/2"

⑬

July Stars & Stripes Oven Mitt

Patriotic red, white and blue make this oven mitt a July 4th hit.

Project Specifications
Pot Holder Size: 8" x 11 1/2"

Fabric
- 1 strip gold solid 1 1/4" x 12"
- 6 1/2" x 8 1/2" rectangle navy print
- 1/3 yard each red and white solids
- 2 rectangles cotton batting 10" x 13"
- 1/2 yard self-made or purchased navy bias binding

Tools & Supplies
- White and navy all-purpose thread
- White machine-embroidery thread
- White quilting thread
- Clear nylon monofilament
- 5" x 5" square fusible transfer web
- 5" x 5" square fabric stabilizer
- Basic sewing tools and supplies

Instructions
1. Prepare template for star shape using pattern piece given. Prepare piece for appliqué referring to the Fusible Appliqué instructions in the General Instructions.

2. Prepare template for mitt cuff shape using pattern given.

3. Fuse star shape to the mitt cuff shape referring to pattern for placement. Machine-appliqué star in place using white machine-embroidery thread and referring to the General Instructions.

4. Sew the gold solid strip to one angled side of the mitt cuff shape; press seams toward gold strip. Trim ends even with mitt cuff as shown in Figure 1. Sew the remainder of the strip to the opposite angled side; press and trim as before. Press raw edge under on gold strip 1/4".

Figure 1
Trim ends even with
mitt cuff as shown.

5. Cut two strips each red and white solids 1 1/4" by fabric width. Sew a white strip to a red strip with right sides together along length; press seams toward red strip. Repeat for two strip sets. Cut into seven 9" segments; join the segments to create a red-and-white-stripe section as shown in Figure 2.

9"

Figure 2
Join the segments to create
a red-and-white-stripe
section.

6. Pin the mitt cuff to one shorter side of the striped section as shown in Figure 3. Using mitt pattern given on pages 10 and 11, adjust mitt cuff on stripe section and cut mitt shape.

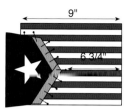

Figure 3
Pin the mitt cuff to 1 shorter side of the stripe section as shown.

7. Topstitch gold strip to stripe section as shown in Figure 4. Using this completed mitt as a pattern, cut two white solid, one red solid and two batting pieces.

Figure 4
Topstitch gold strip to stripe section as shown.

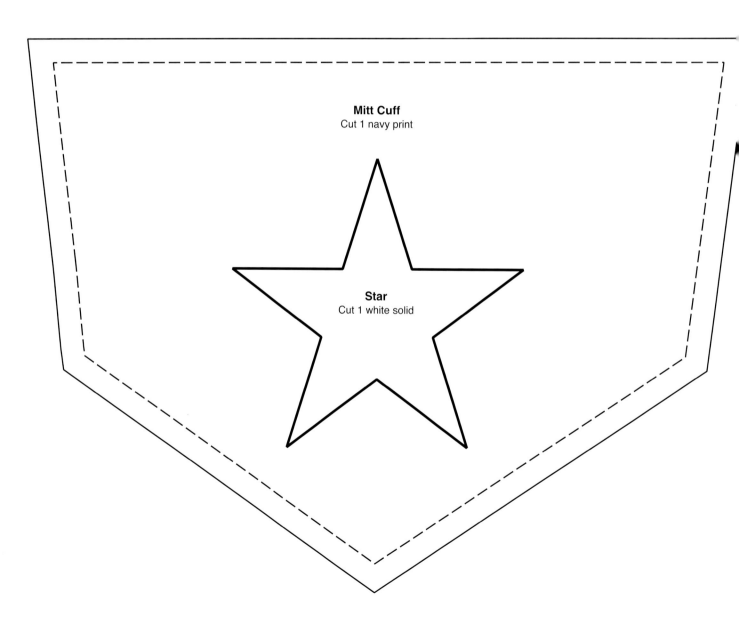

Mitt Cuff
Cut 1 navy print

Star
Cut 1 white solid

8. Draw diagonal lines 1 1/2" apart on one white solid mitt shape in both directions to make a grid as shown in Figure 5. Sandwich a batting piece between the white solid and red solid mitt shapes.

Figure 5
Draw diagonal lines 1 1/2" apart on
the back white mitt in both directions
to make a grid as shown.

9. Using white all-purpose thread, machine-stitch on marked lines.

10. Sandwich the remaining batting piece between the appliquéd mitt top and another white solid lining piece; pin to hold. Hand-quilt 1/4" away from appliquéd star and mitt cuff seam line using white quilting thread. Machine-quilt in the ditch of seams of gold strip and stripe section using clear nylon monofilament in the top of the machine and white all-purpose thread in the bobbin.

11. Place the two quilted mitt shapes with wrong sides together; stitch around sides, leaving top edge open, using a 1/8" seam. Turn wrong side out; stitch around outside edges again using a 1/4" seam and leaving top edges open. **Note:** *This makes a seam enclosed in a seam—a French seam.*

12. Bind the top edge, making a loop referring to the General Instructions to finish. ❖

Stars & Stripes Oven Mitt
Placement Diagram
8" x 11 1/2"

August Harvest Pot Holder

Individual vegetable shapes combine to create an unusual shape on this Harvest pot holder.

Project Specifications

Pot Holder Size: 9 1/2" x 9"

Fabric

- Scraps red, orange and burgundy solids, brown, orange, burgundy, yellow and dark, medium and light green prints and dark green and gold mottleds
- 11" x 11" square white solid
- Cotton batting 11" x 11"

Tools & Supplies

- White all-purpose thread
- Black quilting thread
- Clear nylon monofilament
- 1/2 yard 1/8"-wide green satin ribbon
- Freezer paper
- 1/4 yard fabric stabilizer
- Basic sewing tools and supplies, stylet, knitting needle or pencil, water-erasable fabric marker or pencil and crewel needle with large eye

Instructions

1. Prepare pieces for appliqué referring to Freezer-Paper Appliqué in the General Instructions and referring to pattern pieces for color of fabrics to cut. Reverse each piece before cutting freezer-paper shapes. **Note:** *Use shapes given to cut freezer-paper pieces. Cut each fabric piece 1/4" beyond edge of freezer-paper shape for seam allowance.*

2. Using pot holder pattern for a guide, arrange the vegetables in numerical order and appliqué in place, again referring to the General Instructions.

3. Cut a light green bias strip 2 1/2" x 5" from the light green print; fold in half and press. Fold the two raw edges inside toward the fold; press. Topstitch the strip with white thread close to the edge. Fold the strip into a loop and pin the raw ends to the top of the lettuce piece as marked on pattern.

4. Cut two 8" pieces 1/8"-wide green satin ribbon for tomato stems. Using crewel needle, make three straight stitches on each tomato as marked on pattern, beginning and ending ribbon in the seam allowance; baste across ends to secure.

5. Unfold seam allowance around outside edge of pot holder top; press flat.

6. Cut a matching backing piece from white solid and a matching batting piece. Pin the pot holder top to the backing piece, right sides together; pin the batting to the backing piece.

7. Sew around the outside edges using a 1/4" seam allowance, leaving an opening on the carrot edge. Clip curves and indentations and turn right side out.

8. With a stylet, knitting needle or pencil with broken lead, smooth out seams on the inside. Pull the loop up; slipstitch opening closed. Press lightly.

9. Hand-quilt around each shape and along the detail lines on each vegetable using black quilting thread to finish. ❖

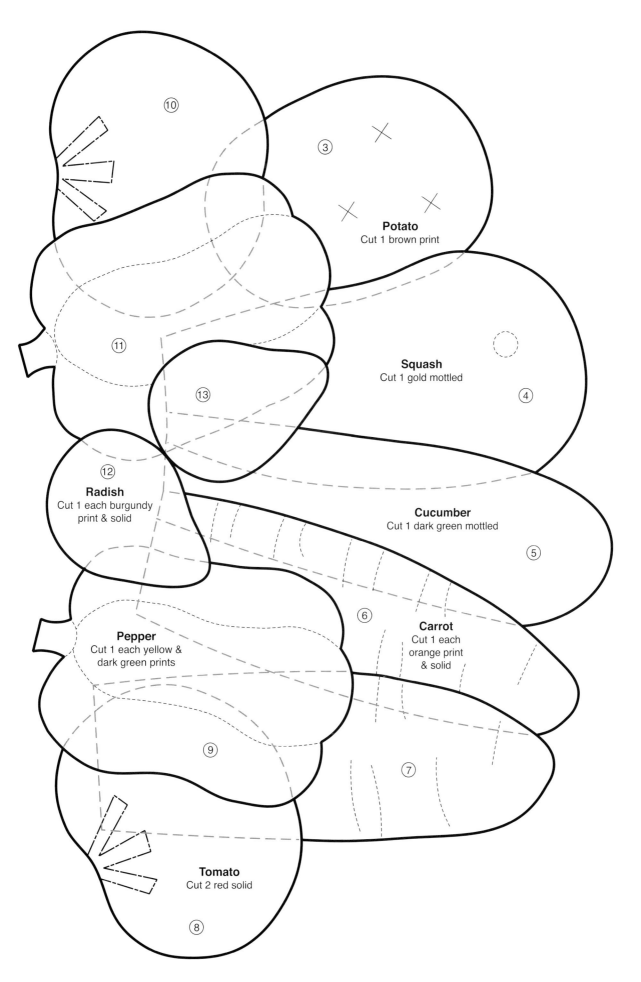

Potato
Cut 1 brown print

Squash
Cut 1 gold mottled

Cucumber
Cut 1 dark green mottled

Carrot
Cut 1 each
orange print
& solid

Radish
Cut 1 each burgundy
print & solid

Pepper
Cut 1 each yellow &
dark green prints

Tomato
Cut 2 red solid

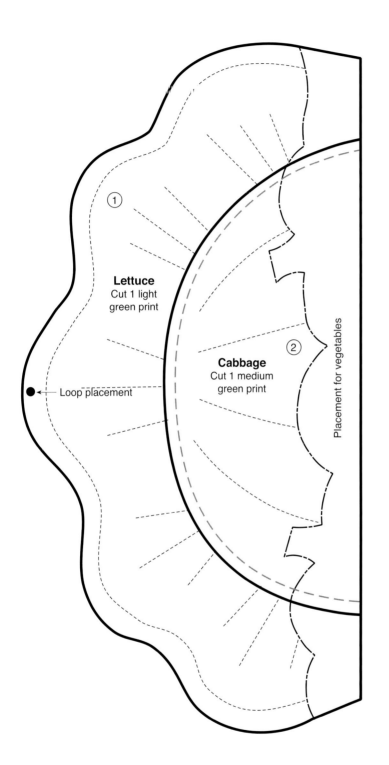

Lettuce
Cut 1 light
green print

Loop placement

Cabbage
Cut 1 medium
green print

Placement for vegetables

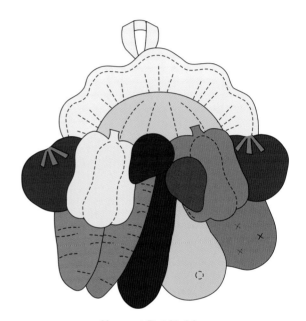

Harvest Pot Holder
Placement Diagram
9 1/2" x 9"

September Log Cabin Apple Pot Holder

Make several of these pot holders to fill a basket with apples near your stove.

Project Specifications

Pot Holder Size: 8 1/4″ x 8″

Fabric

- Scraps 9 different shades red prints, half light and half dark
- 1/8 yard green print
- 10″ x 10″ square red solid for backing
- Cotton batting 14″ x 14″

Tools & Supplies

- Red and green all-purpose thread
- White quilting thread
- Basic sewing tools and supplies and stylet, knitting needle or pencil

Instructions

1. Prepare templates using pattern pieces given. Cut the leaves and apple backing and batting as directed on each piece.

2. Cut one 1 1/2″ x 1 1/2″ square from lightest red print for center. Cut the light and dark red fabrics into 1 1/2″-wide strips.

3. Sew a light strip to the center square, trimming the added strip even with the center square after stitching as shown in Figure 1; press seam toward strip.

4. Continue adding strips and trimming until there are four strips on each side of the center

Figure 1
Sew a strip to the center square, trimming the added strip even with the center square after stitching.

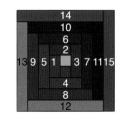

Figure 2
Continue adding strips and trimming until there are 4 strips on each side of the center square to complete a Log Cabin block.

square to complete a Log Cabin block as shown in Figure 2.

5. Using the apple pattern given and referring to lines on the pattern for placement, cut the block even with the pattern.

6. Cut a bias strip 2 1/2″ x 5″ from green print; fold in half and press. Fold the two raw edges inside toward the fold; press. Topstitch the strip with green all-purpose thread close to the edge. Fold the strip into a loop and pin the raw ends to the top center of the apple piece.

7. Pin the pot holder top to the backing piece, right sides together with backing shape; pin the batting to the backing piece.

8. Sew around the outside edges using a 1/4″ seam, leaving an opening as marked on pattern. Clip curves and indentations and turn right side out.

9. With a stylet, knitting needle or pencil with broken lead, smooth out seams on the inside. Pull the loop up; slipstitch opening closed. Press lightly.

10. Hand-quilt in the ditch of seams using white quilting thread.

11. Pin two leaf shapes with right sides together; pin a batting to the wrong side of one leaf shape. Sew around shape, leaving an opening for turning. Trim the points and indentations and clip curves; turn right side out. With a stylet, knitting needle or pencil with broken lead, smooth out seams on

the inside; press lightly. Hand-stitch opening closed. Quilt on marked lines using white quilting thread; repeat for a second leaf unit.

12. Hand-stitch the finished leaf units to the top edge of the finished apple shape referring to placement lines on pattern, leaving edges free to finish. ❖

Log Cabin Apple Pot Holder
Placement Diagram
8 1/4" x 8"

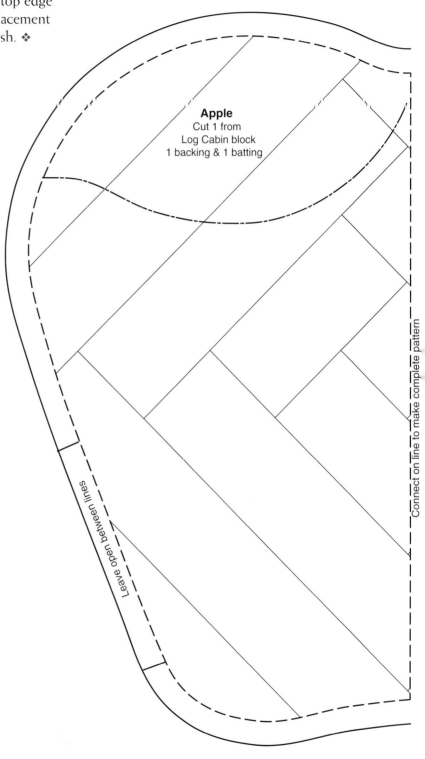

Apple
Cut 1 from
Log Cabin block
1 backing & 1 batting

Connect on line to make complete pattern

Leave open between lines

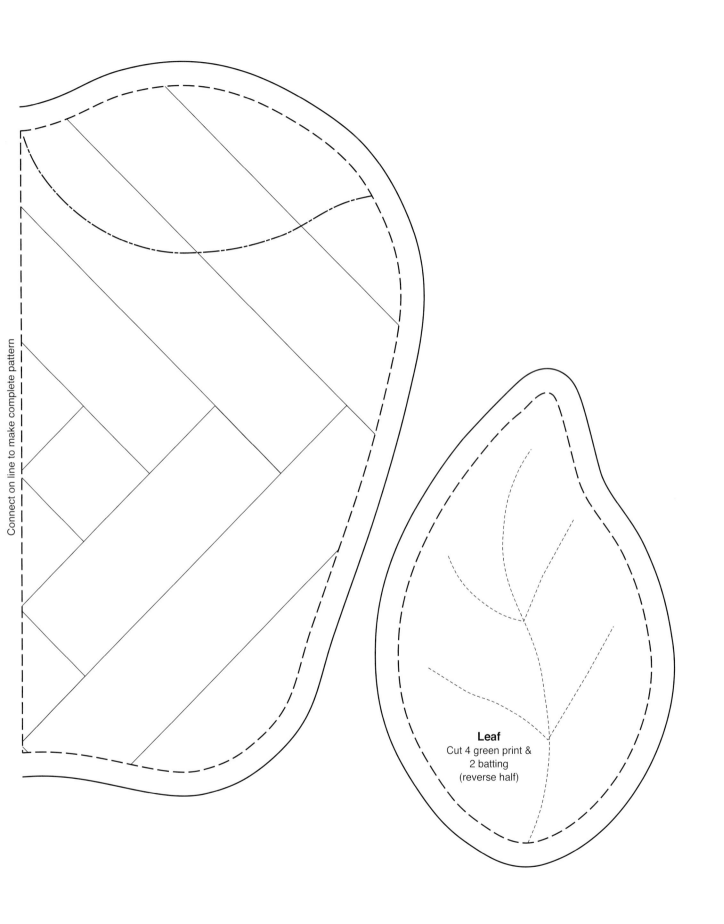

Connect on line to make complete pattern

Leaf
Cut 4 green print &
2 batting
(reverse half)

October Pumpkin Pot Holder

The carved pumpkin shape is a popular symbol of Halloween. Make this neat pot holder to help spook up your kitchen.

Project Specifications
Pot Holder Size: 9 1/4″ x 7 3/4″

Fabric
- Scraps black and yellow print
- 1/8 yard green print
- 1/4 yard orange print
- Cotton batting 8″ x 12″

Tools & Supplies
- Green and orange all-purpose thread
- Black and white quilting thread
- Black machine-embroidery thread
- Clear nylon monofilament
- 1/8 yard fusible transfer web
- 1/4 yard fabric stabilizer
- Basic sewing tools and supplies, stylet, knitting needle or pencil

Instructions
1. Prepare templates using pattern pieces given. Cut the pumpkin and leaf pieces as directed on the patterns. Cut the face pieces and prepare for appliqué referring to Fusible Appliqué in the General Instructions.
2. Transfer detail lines onto the top pumpkin piece.
3. Place face pieces on the top pumpkin piece referring to the pattern for positioning; fuse and stitch in place, again referring to the General Instructions.
4. Cut and pin a piece of fabric stabilizer behind the top pumpkin shape. Using black machine-embroidery thread in the top of the machine and all-purpose thread in the bobbin, machine satin-stitch around all fused shapes; when stitching is complete, remove stabilizer.

5. Pin two leaf shapes with right sides together; pin a batting to the wrong side of one leaf shape. Sew around shape and leave an opening for turning. Trim the points, indentations and clip curves; turn right side out. With a stylet, knitting needle or pencil with broken lead, smooth out seams on the inside; press lightly. Hand-stitch opening closed. Quilt on marked lines using white quilting thread; repeat for a second leaf unit.
6. Cut a bias strip 2 1/2″ x 5″ from green print; fold in half and press. Fold the two raw edges inside toward the fold; press. Topstitch the strip with green thread close to the edge. Fold the strip into a loop and pin the raw ends to the top center of the pumpkin piece.
7. Pin the pot holder top to the backing piece, right sides together with backing shape; pin the batting to the backing piece.
8. Sew around the outside edges using a 1/4″ seam, leaving an opening as marked on pattern. Clip curves and indentations and turn right side out.
9. With a stylet, knitting needle or pencil with broken lead, smooth out seams on the inside. Pull the loop up; slipstitch opening closed. Press lightly.
10. Machine-quilt around appliquéd shapes using clear nylon monofilament in the top of the machine and all-purpose thread in the bobbin. Hand-quilt on marked detail lines using black quilting thread.

11. Hand-stitch the finished leaf units to the top edge of the finished pumpkin shape referring to placement lines on pattern, leaving edges free to finish. ❖

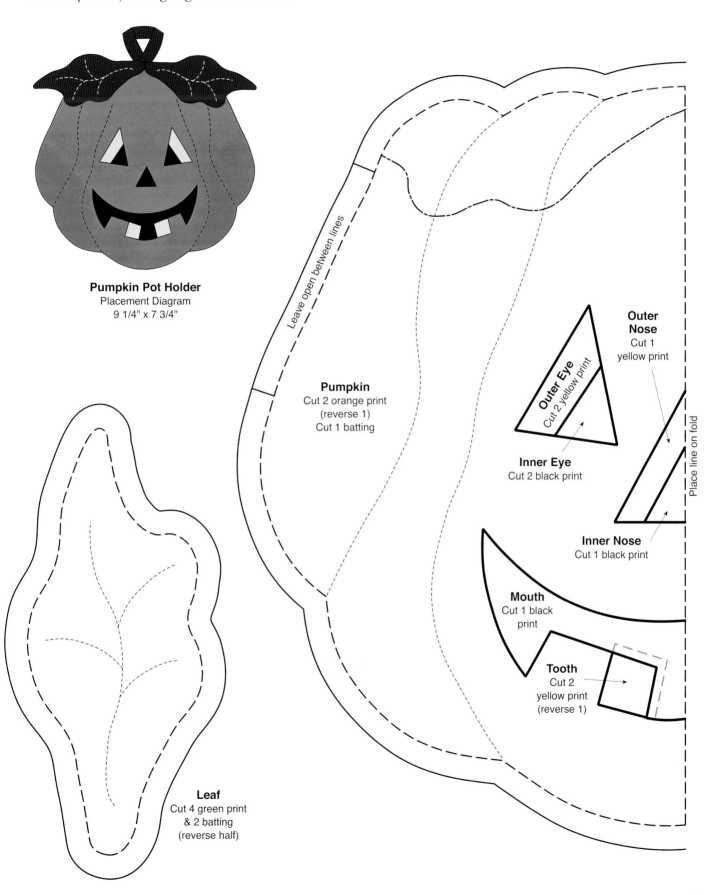

Pumpkin Pot Holder
Placement Diagram
9 1/4" x 7 3/4"

Leave open between lines

Pumpkin
Cut 2 orange print
(reverse 1)
Cut 1 batting

Outer Eye
Cut 2 yellow print

Outer Nose
Cut 1
yellow print

Inner Eye
Cut 2 black print

Place line on fold

Inner Nose
Cut 1 black print

Mouth
Cut 1 black
print

Tooth
Cut 2
yellow print
(reverse 1)

Leaf
Cut 4 green print
& 2 batting
(reverse half)

November Pilgrim Pot Holder

This smiling Pilgrim looks ready for his Thanksgiving meal.

Project Specifications

Pot Holder Size: 8" x 8"

Fabric

- Scraps black, white, brown and peach solids
- 4 squares brown print 1 3/4" x 1 3/4"
- 1 strip orange print 1 3/4" x 28"
- 6" x 6" square off-white solid
- Backing 8 1/2" x 8 1/2"
- Cotton batting 8 1/2" x 8 1/2"
- 1 1/8 yards self-made or purchased dark brown bias binding

Tools & Supplies

- Dark brown all-purpose thread
- Brown and gold machine-embroidery thread
- Brown quilting thread
- Clear nylon monofilament
- 1/8 yard medium-weight fusible interfacing
- 1/8 yard fabric stabilizer
- Basic sewing tools and supplies, stylet, knitting needle or pencil and water-erasable fabric marker or pencil

Instructions

1. Prepare templates for pilgrim motif using pattern given; cut as directed on the pattern.

2. Prepare pilgrim motif pieces for appliqué referring to Interfaced Appliqué in the General Instructions.

3. Center and arrange pilgrim pieces on the diagonal center of the 6" x 6" off-white square.

4. Appliqué pilgrim pieces in place in numerical order referring to Interfaced Appliqué in the General Instructions.

5. Machine-stitch detail lines using brown machine-embroidery thread and a satin stitch for belt, hair and hatband and gold machine-embroidery thread for buckles.

6. Sew a 1 3/4" x 6" orange print strip to opposite sides of the appliquéd square; press seams toward strips.

7. Sew a 1 3/4" x 1 3/4" brown print square to each end of the remaining orange print strips; sew these strips to the remaining sides of the appliquéd square. Press seams toward strips.

8. Prepare for quilting and quilt referring to the General Instructions using brown quilting thread for hand quilting.

9. Bind edges, making a hanging loop, referring to the General Instructions. ❖

Pilgrim Pot Holder
Placement Diagram
8" x 8"

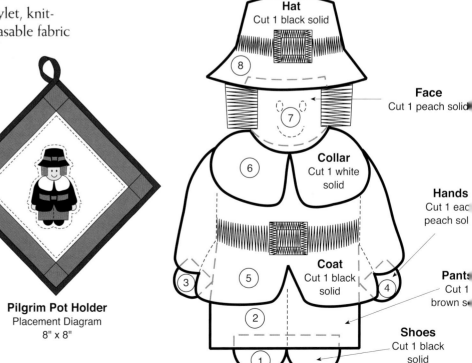

December Santa Pot Holder

Display your December pot holder along with your other holiday decorations during this Christmas season.

Project Specifications
Pot Holder Size: 8" x 8 3/4"

Fabric
- Scraps green, dark green, brown, peach and yellow prints
- Scraps red and white solid
- 1/4 yard dark green solid
- Cotton batting 10" x 10"
- 1 1/4 yards self-made or purchased red bias binding

Tools & Supplies
- Neutral color all-purpose thread
- White quilting thread
- Green, white, yellow, brown, black and red machine-embroidery thread
- Clear nylon monofilament
- 1/4 yard fusible transfer web
- 1/4 yard fabric stabilizer
- Basic sewing tools and supplies

Instructions
1. Prepare templates using pattern pieces given. Cut the pot holder pieces as directed on the pattern. Cut the appliqué pieces and prepare for appliqué referring to Fusible Appliqué in the General Instructions.

2. Place appliqué pieces on one pot holder piece referring to the pattern for positioning; fuse and stitch in place with matching machine-embroidery thread, again referring to the General Instructions. Add bag tie lines using yellow machine-embroidery thread, eyes using black machine-embroidery thread and a mouth using red machine-embroidery thread.

3. Prepare for quilting and quilt referring to the General Instructions using white quilting thread for hand quilting.

4. Bind edges, making a hanging loop, referring to the General Instructions to finish. ❖

Santa Pot Holder
Placement Diagram
8" x 8 3/4"

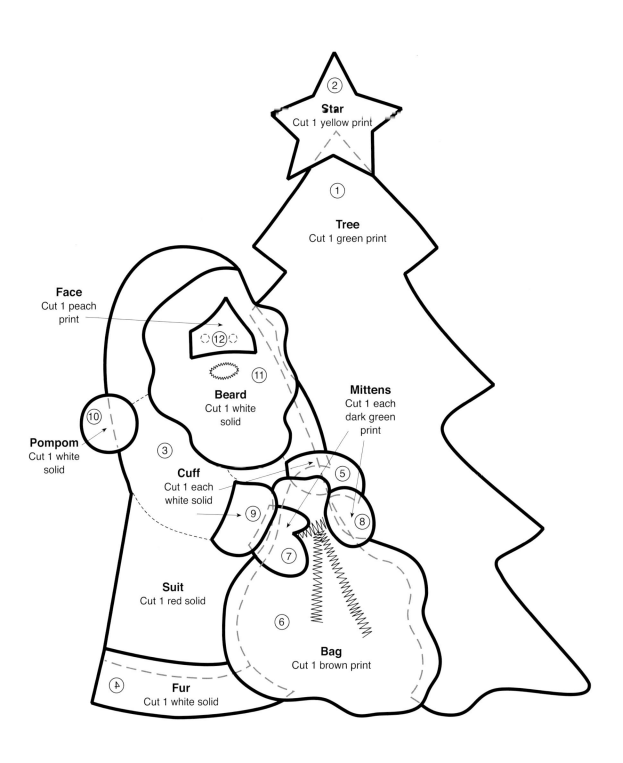

Star
Cut 1 yellow print

Tree
Cut 1 green print

Face
Cut 1 peach
print

Beard
Cut 1 white
solid

Mittens
Cut 1 each
dark green
print

Pompom
Cut 1 white
solid

Cuff
Cut 1 each
white solid

Suit
Cut 1 red solid

Bag
Cut 1 brown print

Fur
Cut 1 white solid

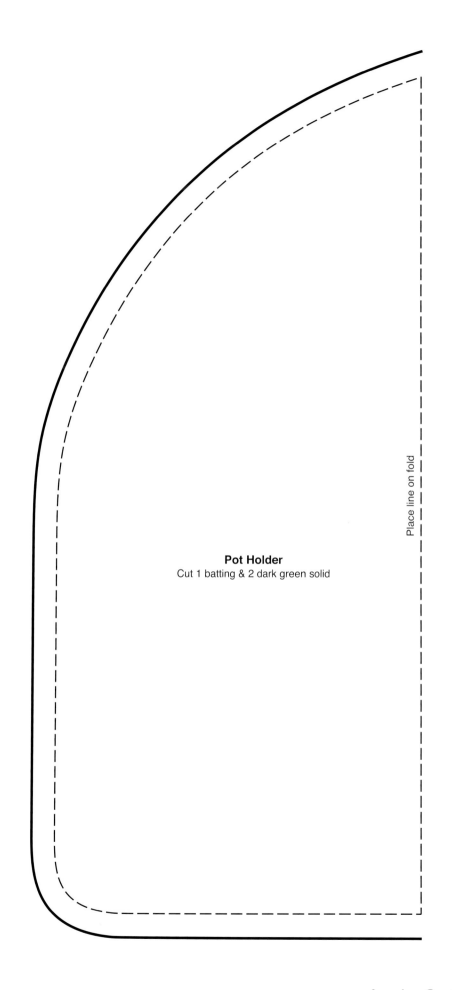

Pot Holder
Cut 1 batting & 2 dark green solid

Place line on fold